Ladder Books

Edited by Olive Robinson

KU-356-780

Birds

by J. Thorogood

© Oxford University Press, 1976

Oxford University Press 1976

Mating

Golden orioles. The male
is a brighter yellow than
the female

1   Have you seen birds making nests in the spring? Before they do this, a male and female of the same kind must join up to make a pair. The male chases the female and jumps on top of her. Then he puts a special kind of seed called sperm into her, which will make young birds grow in the eggs she lays. This is called mating.

2   Most male birds look brighter than females. This attracts the females to them for mating. The picture of a pair of golden orioles shows you how different male and female birds can be.

3   The male works hard to find his mate. He must have a territory before a female will join him. This territory can be one tree, or part of a river bank, or just a small patch of ground. Sometimes he fights to protect it from other males of his kind. Often he just sings or makes signals with his body and wings. This warns other male birds to keep away.

4   When he has a territory he must still get a female to mate with him. Some kinds of birds make a display. This is their way of showing off their good looks. A peacock lifts his long tail up and spreads it like a fan. Many parks and zoos have peacocks and you can see a picture of one on page 22.

A male prairie chicken in his mating dance

5   The picture above shows a prairie chicken from North America. Its display is like a strange dance. It blows out orange bags of skin under its cheek and jumps up and down, making loud booming noises.

6   Sometimes 2 males try to attract the same female and they may end up fighting for her. Male pheasants often fight in the mating season. They fluff out their feathers and fly at each other, pecking and scratching, but they do not kill each other. The golden pheasants below come from China.

Golden pheasants. You can see which one is the male

Nesting

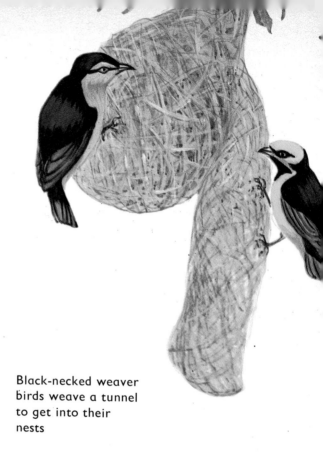

1   When 2 birds have mated they build a nest, where the female lays her eggs. Some kinds of birds, like pigeons, lay only 1 or 2 eggs. Others, like pheasants, can lay more than 10 eggs. Most birds lay between 4 and 8 eggs. Often the mother sits on the eggs to keep them warm, until they hatch. Then the parents are busy finding food for the hungry young birds.

Black-necked weaver birds weave a tunnel to get into their nests

2   Have you looked into a bird's nest? This is hard to do, because birds build nests to protect their eggs and young from enemies, like rats or people. Mostly they build them where you cannot see or touch them. They are hard to see because they look like the things all round them. Nests in trees are made of twigs, and nests near the ground are made of grass and moss. Many birds put mud or feathers round the inside of their nests to make them warm. Most nests are cup-shaped, but some have special shapes, like the black-necked weaver's nest in the picture. Some kinds of weaver birds join their nests together in one group. Then the birds look after each other's nests.

3   The cave swiftlet of Borneo makes a nest of its own spit on the walls of caves. Chinese people buy these nests for making soup! The spotted woodpeckers in the picture have found a hole in a tree and have made it bigger with their beaks. Birds that live near houses may make nests under roofs, as sparrows and house martins do. Others make nests in old pipes or kettles, as robins sometimes do.

Woodpeckers make their nests in hollow trees

4   Some birds, that live in places where there are not many people, lay their eggs in the open. Seagulls lay their eggs on cliff-tops and rocky ledges where it is dangerous for people to go. Grouse and partridge live on moors and fields, and lay their eggs in small hollows in the grass or heather.

A meadow pipit feeding a young cuckoo

5   The cuckoo does not build a nest at all. It lays an egg in another bird's nest. Then it leaves the other bird to hatch the egg and feed the baby. In the bottom picture the big bird is the young cuckoo. It has pushed the meadow pipit's own babies out of the nest. The pipit has to work hard to feed its big hungry foster child.

Singing

A thrush repeats parts of its song over and over again.

1   Every bird has its own kind of call. Next time you hear a bird, listen to it carefully. If you can see it, notice its shape and colour. Then look for its picture in a bird book and find out what kind it is. One of the best singers is the thrush. It has a short song which it repeats often. It also has a call which has one note only. Many birds use these calls to warn each other of danger.

A nightingale sings as night falls

2   You can read on page 1 how some male birds sing to protect their territory and attract their mates. Most songs are heard in spring and summer when the birds are mating and nesting. Most birds start singing very early in the morning, and this is the best time to hear them. But the nightingale goes on singing after dark, when most other birds have stopped. It sings in storms too

3   In the country you can often hear a skylark. It sings as it flies up high into the sky, so high that you can hardly see it. Its happy song goes on and on. Birds sing loudly so that they can be heard from far away. A wren is less than 10 centimetres long, and it is always a surprise to hear its loud song.

A wren

4   Some birds, like canaries, know what to sing by instinct. This means that they will sing canary songs even if they never hear them from another canary. Other birds, like chaffinches and bullfinches, learn their songs from their fathers. Some birds can learn other songs as well. People used to keep bullfinches (see the picture on page 12) to teach them new tunes.

5   Some birds have strange songs. Starlings can copy many sounds. One morning you may think you can hear the milkman whistling and then you find it was only a starling! Mocking-birds from North America copy other birds' songs. They even learned the song of some English nightingales that were taken to America in cages. An Australian bird, the kookaburra, sounds like someone laughing. This is why it is often called the laughing jackass.

Mocking-birds copy the songs of other birds. Unlike many birds, they sing all the year round

Feeding

A golden eagle easily kills rabbits with its beak and claws

1   Birds spend most of their time looking for food. The golden eagle is a very big bird which eats other birds and animals. Because of this, it is called a bird of prey. Golden eagles are nearly a metre long and they have sharp hooked beaks and claws. They can even kill young lambs. There are eagles in most countries. One of the biggest is the wedge-tailed eagle of Australia.

2   Most birds of prey are smaller than eagles. Barn owls, which live in many parts of the world, eat rats and mice. They hunt at night, and their flight is soft and silent. Owls have very good eyes for seeing in the dark.

3 The Peking robin in the picture is just going to eat an insect. Most insect-eaters catch their food in the air as they fly. Look out for swallows on a warm summer evening. You may see them flying near the ground, twisting and turning quickly as they chase insects that you can hardly see.

A Peking robin from China

4 Many birds feed on seeds. If you see small birds with feathers of gold, red, and black flying round thistles in autumn, they are goldfinches. In the picture on page 12 you can see they have strong beaks for eating hard seeds.

A humming-bird has a long thin beak for putting into flowers to get nectar

5 Humming-birds, which live in the warm parts of America, have a strange way of feeding. They suck the sweet nectar out of flowers while they hover still in the air—almost like tiny helicopters.

6 Most birds have their own favourite kind of food. But all of them will eat almost anything when they are hungry. Seagulls follow ships, hoping for scraps of food. In winter, hungry ducks will rush from ponds and rivers to take bread from you.

Beaks and feet

An eagle's beak is made for tearing

A nightjar's beak opens very wide

A flamingo's beak is like a strainer

1   Every bird has a special kind of beak to help it eat its own kind of food. Look at the 3 drawings above. The eagle's beak is sharp and hooked for tearing flesh from the body of its prey. The nightjar's beak looks tiny when it is shut. But when it flies, it opens its beak so wide that it is like a net to catch insects. The flamingo's beak works like a strainer. It is used for straining tiny animals out of muddy water.

An oyster catcher digging in the sand

2   Herons have long sharp beaks which they use like spears for catching and killing their food. They stand still and silent in shallow water and then jab suddenly when they see fish or eels. Other birds use long beaks for digging in sand and mud. The oyster catcher in the picture digs for small shell-fish and other animals along the sea-shore.

3 All birds that perch need long, thin toes that curl round thin twigs. Look at the marsh tit in the picture. Can you see that one toe of each foot bends back, away from the others, like your thumb? This gives the bird a strong grip. Birds with feet like this sometimes use them for holding food while they eat.

Notice how the marsh tit uses its toes to perch on a twig

4 At the bottom of the page you can see how different birds' feet are made to help them. The lily-trotter, which lives in hot countries, has wide feet. These spread its weight so that it will not sink when it walks on water plants. The sea eagle has such strong, sharp claws that it can kill fish by crushing them. The last drawing shows the webbed feet of a shag. The shag spends most of its life swimming. Its toes are joined by a web of skin so that its feet are like paddles pushing it through the water. Most other swimming birds, like swans, ducks, and geese, also have webbed feet.

A lily-trotter's toes spread its weight

Eagles kill small animals with their claws

Webbed feet help birds to swim fast

Feathers and colours

1   To a bird, feathers are more than just its 'clothes'. Without feathers, it could not fly, and it would not find a mate. So birds take good care of their feathers. Have you seen birds splashing about in puddles? After a bath like this many birds finish cleaning themselves by scratching and rubbing their feathers with their heads and beaks. This is called preening. But every bird has feathers, like the ones on its head, that it cannot reach easily. So, many birds help to preen each other, and you may see them helping to keep each other clean like this.

2   Look at the birds at the top of the next page. Each one has its special colours and markings. These help the birds to find others of the same kind—which is very important for mating (see page 1). All these birds have white markings on their backs or their wings, and these show up clearly when they fly up suddenly. It can be a warning of danger to other birds.

3   Feathers can also help a bird to hide from its enemies. Ptarmigans live in the dark heather on hills in Scotland, and in summer they are brown. But in winter, when snow covers the hills, the ptarmigan has white feathers that help to hide it in the snow.

The ptarmigan goes white in winter

Bullfinch

Australian robin

Chaffinch

4   Most young birds have dull feathers that help them to hide while they are too young to escape from their enemies by flying. On page 2, the male pheasant at the bottom of the page is easy to see, but the young chicks are hard to find. By the time they have bright feathers, the young birds have learned to fly from danger. Then, every year, birds slowly lose their feathers—while new ones grow to take their place. This is called moulting, but mostly it happens too slowly for us to notice.

5   Why don't ducks catch cold? Have you ever wondered how they keep warm in ponds and lakes? Most water-birds have a kind of oil that comes from under their tails. They rub it over themselves while they are preening. This makes their feathers water-proof. So birds like the diver in the picture below can spend their time in the water, but always stay warm and dry.

The colour of the red-throated diver makes it hard to see against the water

Wings and flying

The long wings of these Manx
shearwaters help them to glide

1 The most important
feathers for flying are the
ones on a bird's wing. The
tiny hair-like parts of a
wing-feather can open to
let air through or they can
close to push against the
air and lift the bird up.
Nearly all birds fly, but
different kinds of birds
fly in different ways.

2 Manx shearwaters fly over the
sea for most of the time, looking for
fish. They would get tired if they had to
flap their wings all the time so they fly
up high and then hold their wings out
straight. They glide down out of the sky
and nearly skim the sea before they
flap their wings to fly up high again.

3 Eagles stay in the air for a long
time while they hunt for food. The
picture shows that an eagle's wings are
very long and wide. They are made for
soaring. Eagles keep their wings spread
out and still, and they let the wind
lift them high around the mountains
where they live.

Eagles can fly faster
than almost any other
birds with their
big powerful wings

4. Many birds spend most of the time on the ground or perched in trees. They fly only a little way from one tree to another. Most of these birds have short wings which they flap quite fast. Many small birds, like blue tits and robins, have wings like this.

A robin has to flutter its small wings fast

5 Some birds, like the kestrel, can hover on their long, pointed wings. Kestrels stay still in the air, by making tiny fast movements with their wings and spreading out their tail feathers. This means that they can watch one small patch of ground. When they see a mouse or a small bird below them, they suddenly fold their wings and drop on to it like a stone. You can often see kestrels hovering over grass by the side of motor-ways.

6 Birds make flying look so easy that some people have tried to copy them. They have tied home-made wings to their arms. But no man can lift himself off the ground in this way. It is easy for birds because they have hollow bones that make them very light. They also have very strong muscles in their chests. They need these to flap their wings hard enough to carry themselves through the air.

Migration

1   Every year, some kinds of birds leave the country where they were born and fly somewhere else for the winter. This is called migration. Swallows come to Europe in spring and summer, when they breed and find many insects to eat. In the autumn, when days are colder, they may fly to South Africa, over 9,000 kilometres away. There it is spring, and there will be plenty of food for them.

Swallows

2   Late in summer, you can see big flocks of birds getting ready to migrate. Most migrating birds fly at night, and rest and feed in the daytime. But birds that catch their food in the air migrate in the daytime, when there are insects about. The arctic tern in the picture breeds in the far north, often near Greenland. At the end of summer it flies about 15,000 kilometres to its other home near the South Pole. You can see where it goes on the map in the front of this book.

The arctic tern migrates between the north and the south ends of the world. On the 2 journeys it may fly 30,000 kilometres or more

3   Some birds migrate on nearly the same day every year.
Other birds wait longer if the weather is good. But all birds
seem to know when and where to go. Even young birds can find
their way on long journeys. Some birds come back to the same
nesting place every year after flying thousands of kilometres.
We know that some birds are helped by seeing where the sun and
stars are in the sky. Because of this, migrating birds may get
lost in foggy or cloudy weather.

4   If you look at the map in the front you will see some
interesting things. Birds that get their food from the sea—
like the arctic tern—migrate over water, even when this makes
their journey longer. Other birds, like spine-tailed swifts, eat
insects that live over land. So when the swifts migrate over the
sea, they fly from island to island to find their food.

5   Some birds, like the
American plover, leave their
breeding grounds by one way
and go back a different way.
White storks migrate from
Europe to a number of
places—some to Africa,
others to northern India.

A white stork. The map
in the front of the book
shows the different
places that storks
migrate to

6   Not all birds migrate.
Birds like robins and tits stay
in the same place and change
their food as the seasons
change. In summer tits live on
insects, but in winter they
eat seeds and berries.

Birds that cannot fly

1   The birds in these pictures cannot fly. Most of them can run fast, so they do not need to fly to escape from their enemies. Some are so big and strong that not many animals dare to attack them. Penguins are slow on their feet, but they are very good swimmers and so they are mostly safe when they are in the water.

2   The cassowary from Australia is about 150 centimetres tall—nearly as tall as a man. It feeds at night, and lives in thick thorn bushes. On its wings are strong spikes and it uses these to tear a path through the bushes. The kiwi from New Zealand is much smaller. It is a night bird and hides in a burrow, or hole, in the day. It can run fast if it is in danger.

The cassowary is big and strong enough to defend itself well

A kiwi from New Zealand

3   Ostriches are giant birds, about 240 centimetres tall. They live on the plains of Africa. There are ostrich farms in Africa where the farmers breed them to sell their beautiful feathers. Ostriches lay their eggs in hollows which they make in the ground. They have the biggest eggs in the world—about 20 centimetres long. When they hatch, the chicks are already 30 centimetres tall. When they are a year old they can run at nearly 50 kilometres an hour. An ostrich can kick like a horse if it is attacked.

4   The penguin's short legs are no good for running but when it is in the water it swims very fast, using its wings as paddles. Penguins live close together in huge groups. This helps to defend them from their enemies like skuas—big sea-birds that attack young penguins. There are penguins in South Africa and Australia, but most of them live in the cold, icy far south of the world.

A family of penguins

An ostrich and its new chick

Birds in the garden

1   How many kinds of birds can you see round your house? Even if you have only a small back yard, birds will come to it. Robins, chaffinches, blue tits, and great tits are used to people. Blue tits often drink milk on doorsteps by pecking through milk-bottle tops—mostly in winter. Other birds, like thrushes and blackbirds, come to eat worms and snails. Starlings come in flocks and often chase other birds away from the food that you put out. And near most houses you will find sparrows. All these birds come for food that they can find round houses and gardens.

2   In the winter, birds cannot find food easily. So if you put crumbs and fat outside, you will see birds that do not come close to houses in the summer. Greenfinches might come to eat bread. If there are old trees near your house, you may see spotted woodpeckers. They come to eat insects that live in the bark of the trees.

woodpecker

greenfinch

chaffinch

blue tit

3   On pages 7 and 8 you can read about the different kinds of food that birds like. They also feed in different ways. Why not have a bird-table in your garden? The bird-table in the picture is easy to make. Make it too high for cats to jump on to, and put it away from fences and trees. Put a roof over it to keep the food dry. Give the birds something to perch on, because their feet are made for holding on to branches.

4   Tits like nuts and bacon rind and pieces of fat. You can hang these on string round your table. Bird seed from shops is a good food for finches. In winter, birds will eat almost anything left over from your meals. Put out some clean water in a bowl every day. Birds like to drink and have a bath even in cold weather!

robin

great tit

5   Would you like birds to make nests in your garden? You can help them if you fix a nesting-box in a safe place, out of reach of cats. In a year or two, robins or blue tits may build a nest there. If this happens, do not upset the birds by going too close to their nest, or you will frighten them away.

6   You can buy nesting-boxes from the Royal Society for the Protection of Birds, The Lodge, Sandy, Bedfordshire. You could write a letter to ask them more about looking after birds.

Birds as pets

1   One of the most popular pets is the budgie, which is what we call the budgerigar. They come from Australia, and are friendly little birds with bright feathers of blue, yellow, or green. Parrots, like the one in the picture, can also be good pets. They can learn to say words, and they are good at copying other birds—and other noises too. Parrots come from hot countries, so, if you have one as a pet, you must keep it warm.

A parrot uses its claws and beak for climbing branches

2   Some birds are kept as pets because they sing so well. The best pet singing birds are canaries. They get their name from the Canary Islands where they live wild. The ones you see in pet shops are mostly born in cages. People used to catch wild birds, like bullfinches and linnets, to keep as pets. These birds often died because they could not live in little cages. It was a cruel thing to do, and now some countries have laws to stop people catching wild birds and keeping them in cages.

3   In parks and large gardens you can see birds like ducks, swans, and geese. They walk and swim about as if they were wild, but they do not fly away. They trust people to take care of them. In some parks there are peacocks, like the one in the picture below. On page 2 you can read how they can spread their tails, to attract a female.

4   Birds make interesting pets. But you must take great care of them. Buy pets from people who know about them. They will tell you how to look after them. Get the biggest cage you can buy, because even tame birds need to stretch their wings. Give your bird food and water every day and remember to keep it warm. You could go to your library, and ask for books about keeping birds as pets.

A peacock. A long time ago people used to keep them for food

Index

The number of the page is in black; the number of the paragraph is in red.

Printed in Gt. Britain by W S Cowell Ltd.